FEATHERS FOR DECEMBER

A MONTH OF DIVINE GUIDANCE AND INTUITIVE TEACHINGS

Heather Tobin

Rock Your Mud

Newmarket, Ontario, Canada

Copyright © 2021 by Heather Tobin.

All rights reserved. No part of this publication may be reproduced, distributed or transmitted in any form or by any means, including photocopying, recording, or other electronic or mechanical methods, without the prior written permission of the publisher, except in the case of brief quotations embodied in critical reviews and certain other noncommercial uses permitted by copyright law.

Heather Tobin/Rock Your Mud

Feathers for December/Heather Tobin —1st ed.

ISBN 978-1-7774410-2-9

Dedicated to the Believers.

INTRODUCTION

Have you ever noticed how feathers appear with a special kind of gentleness, usually as a sign and carrying a message from Spirit?

They greet us gracefully and when we watch them float down and come to rest wherever they land, we often experience a certain kind of quiet all around.

Or maybe you're like me when you see one and you feel a slight catch in your throat as you take a shortened breath. Or maybe you feel peaceful energy around you and in that brief moment you have a small inkling, a tiny whisper, or gentle goosebumps, that remind you all is well and will be okay.

One of my wishes is for people to feel comforted, safe and loved. I also want people to know they are protected and divinely guided always.

This led me to think of some possible ways this could be done. How might I create and deliver something simple and just enough?

Feathers for December was born.

A daily message inspired by channeled guidance from Spirit, as well as my own experiences during December in 2020.

This book is an invitation to slowly savour the messages one at a time for a daily dose of comfort or immerse yourself in an afternoon of spiritual solace. You could even flip to a random page and see what Spirit wants you to know in that moment.

May you become aware of all the Feather messages in your life and may this book serve you well.

DECEMBER 1, 2020

"I tried going against my own soul's warning
But in the end, something just didn't feel right."

("My Own Soul's Warning" by The Killers,
Songwriter: Brandon Flowers)

Hello December.

The snow was a delight to see this morning. Undisturbed, still softly falling while I looked outside long before the rest of the neighbourhood woke.

It's the start of a new month. Beginnings always feel so good to me. A clean page in my planner (stationery lover supreme), an energetic wave of newness and the sense that I get to take what I learned from last month and see what I can do better this month.

What I also know is that new beginnings can start at any time. They don't need to be on a Monday, the beginning of a new month or on the infamous January 1st.

A beginning is whenever you decide one should start.

Each moment and each breath are opportunities to press the reset button and begin again.

I also know it can be hard if we are in some sort of pain or struggle, to remember that each new moment is a potential fresh start.

As I was trying to collect myself last night to prepare for this first message for today, I couldn't quite find the words. For hours, I didn't know what I wanted the first message to be.

It was because I wasn't connected to my soul space of knowing, and I had to honour my struggling brain exactly where she was.

My husband shared a piece of writing with me from *"Dear Leader: My Escape from North Korea" by Jang Jin-sung.*

"A piece of writing will stubbornly pause its author and hold him accountable to the end. Look to your conscience; speak your own truth. That is the only way that you can go beyond what you have been taught and accomplish a literature that truly belongs to you."

When I find myself in moments of fog, it's because I'm pushing. The silence is my warning that it's time to put whatever I am working on to rest and return to it when I'm connected to my inner knowing. I had to walk away and wait for the moment to begin again.

What do you need to walk away from so that you can begin again?

DECEMBER 2, 2020

CELEBRATIONS

It is exactly one month before my birthday. Now, of course, these messages aren't about *me*... but the theme for today's message was inspired by the energy running through my veins.

If you're curious, on January 2nd I will be turning 40 going on about 200 in Spirit years or 10 when it comes to my child-like amusement and high-pitched voice when I am being amused by our Fur-Kid Pinto the Cat.

I didn't always see life as a celebration. For a long time, life was a burden while I drove the struggle bus.

I work daily to maintain a healthy mindset. Sometimes my wiring can get tangled up with old ways, but these days it's usually a quick catch and I'm able to course correct.

When we begin to care for ourselves and approach life in a healthier way, it can take time before it creates a deep enough groove that becomes the new, and true way.

I've arrived at the place of fully believing that if you are here, alive on this planet, then your existence is reason enough to celebrate.

You are magic in motion.

Your body functions without you stopping to think about it. That's rather miraculous in and of itself, don't you think?

You probably did things yesterday or today that you do regularly that you don't stop to think about because they are so habitual and easy for you now, but maybe they once weren't.

Today, on my one-month-pre-birthday-mention (innocent smirk) -- I want to celebrate you!

I want you to know that it doesn't matter what you did in the past, what you think you messed up or if you actually made a big whoopsie and you are still carrying some guilt over it... you're doing just fine. Also, between us? In most cases, you're probably a heck of a lot more epic than you give yourself credit for.

So, wear a party hat today if you feel like it, maybe eat some cake, use the fancy dishes and glasses, put on your favourite outfit just because and know this: you are awesome, so light that fire within and shine your beautiful light wherever you go today.

DECEMBER 3

"Worry is a means of using up the present moment in being consumed about something in the future, over which you have no control." ~Wayne Dyer

Take a breath.

Take another breath.

Allow your shoulders to rest where they belong (not up around your ears).

Release the tension in your belly (yes, all that tightness).

Is that a little better?

It is so easy to slip into a state of worry or find ourselves stressed. It often builds before we notice the tension headache, stomach rumbles or fatigue setting in.

I once heard that worry was like a rocking chair - it didn't get you anywhere. What I've learned is that a rocking chair can be soothing but worrying takes us to no-where-goodville because no amount of worry changes any outcome. It just determines our experience of a situation.

If you feel like you're stuck in a cycle of worry, take yourself off the hook just for a moment. Let yourself have a worry-free day.

Pack up all your worries in a box, put them on the imaginary shelf of your mind and let Source/Spirit/The Universe work their magic with whatever those concerns might be.

Let yourself enjoy a day of peace; the worries of your mind will be there tomorrow if you really want to pick them back up again.

DECEMBER 4, 2020

BUTTERFLIES

They swoop in just when you need them.

Reminding you of gentleness.

Bringing a message of hope to your days.

Always when you need a sign.

A reminder that all is well.

The quiet peaceful energy they bring as they land beside you on a warm summer day.

A kind hello from a passerby and just for a moment, your trust in humanity is restored.

My first tattoo representing my transformation, a butterfly, with the word believe on my ankle.

Our kitty is my butterfly, reminding me to play, rest and not take life so seriously.

My husband is my butterfly, just what I need in any given moment.

Look for the butterflies and if you don't see one, take a look in the mirror, as you may be someone else's butterfly today.

DECEMBER 5, 2020

HOPE

What if just for a moment, you imagined that everything would work out just fine...

or better than fine...

like, great or marvelous?

What if you allowed your mind to hear a different story, as you envisioned the most perfect journey ahead...

What if you allowed yourself to embrace... hope.

H - *hold*
O - *on*
P - *pain*
E - *ends*

Whether it's in body, mind or Spirit, hold on just a little longer and don't give up before the miracle has time to arrive.

DECEMBER 6, 2020

RUFFLED FEATHERS

What do you do when your feathers get ruffled?

Well, naturally, most of us flock to a like-feathered friend and share our woes.

But sometimes, depending on certain friends, they may help keep your feathers ruffled or they may help you to see another perspective.

When you get your feathers ruffled, what would happen if you tried to approach the situation with calmness, clarity and resolution? Rather than making a bigger mess of things and turning the situation into the equivalent of a busted open feather pillow all over your life?

We all get ruffled feathers from time to time, but eventually at some point, a light bulb goes on and we see how our approach defaults us to staying... ruffled.

The next time you find yourself in this position, try the opposite. Find a moment of clarity, look for the silver lining or call the friend who can give you perspective rather than the one who adds more ruffle to your fired-up feathers.

Wishing you an un-ruffled, feathery day.

DECEMBER 7, 2020

"What the world needs now is love, sweet love"

("What the World Needs Now Is Love" by Jackie DeShannon, Songwriters: Hal David / Burt F. Bacharach)

I once enjoyed the sentiment of this song, but what I now believe is that the world doesn't need love - the world IS love.

People are love, all the creatures, the winged ones, the four-legged. The trees, the flowers and the bees.

All love.

You.

Me.

All love.

The world is filled with more love than we can comprehend.

Love is everywhere.

But sometimes we have moments that feel unloving.

Or experiences that leave us feeling unloved.

Or situations where we might believe we are unlovable.

Today, be reminded that you are loved, loving and lovable.

We just forget sometimes and get caught up in the fear of what is going on around us.

Even when you don't feel it or have someone say it to you.

Especially when you don't believe that you are.

The world is filled with love, sweet love. As are you.

DECEMBER 8, 2020

DEAR JOHN

Today, on the 40th Anniversary of John Lennon's death, I don't know how I could pick one single quote to share here with you.

As I read through some of his lyrics, I feel the depth and shed a few tears. To say that he has left a mark is an understatement.

In my office, I have a picture of him and alongside it a wall hanging that reads,

"It matters not
Who you love,
Where you love,
Why you love,
When you love, or
How you love,
It matters only
That you love."

Today, I invite you to find a piece of poetry, a song, an inspiring quote, and feel it with your whole heart in a way you haven't felt it before.

Let the moment leave a mark and inspire today.

DECEMBER 9, 2020

THE BASICS

It seems so obvious and yet, we often forget the basics or we convince ourselves we'll get to them *later*. If you've been waiting since 1999 to get back to the basics, consider this your love note reminder that later has come and gone multiple times.

Today is action day.

Let's keep it simple: pick one action that you can do to take care of your basic needs, that will make for a much better day than had you ignored yourself. Nothing like dehydration to give you a case of the crankies or skipped meals making you hangry.

If you want to go all out, you might even want to say something nice to yourself today. I talk to my plants (and myself) all the time. Give it a whirl…see what basics your heart needs today.

DECEMBER 10, 2020

BREATHE
BREATHE
BREATHE

People often ask what my magical solution is for calming my nerves. So I've outlined my 3 step system above for you.

The 4th step is laughter.

Laughing at the silliness of it all.

Laughing at the madness of it all.

Laughing at how seriously we take ourselves.

Laughing at the fact that we are laughing at nothing and everything all at the same time.

Today, let yourself laugh so hard that you must stop and catch your breath.

Then take those long deep inhales, one at a time.

Breathe

Breathe

Breathe

Better?

DECEMBER 11, 2020

BEGINNINGS AND ENDINGS

We are moving toward the end of a challenging year.

Just like every other year, we have stories to share and moments of some kind that have left a mark. This year feels like it's created deeper grooves in many of our lives.

Some we wish to forget and some we wish to remember forever.

I'm also noticing the similar sentiment from year to year, made by people expressing how thankful they'll be when this year is finally over.

I'm not sure what magical Utopia people are expecting will happen when the clock strikes midnight at the start of the new year, but what I do know is this...

We get tangled up with expectations around beginnings.

We get tangled up with everything to wrap up before *the end*. The end of the day, the week, the month, the year.

How much more relaxed would we be if instead we focused on the sun rising and setting each day? This isn't about sticking our heads in the sand and pretending '2020' didn't happen. It's about defining it in a way that makes it meaningful for us.

What if right now is a beginning?

What if right now is a time to end something?

Remember yesterday we took breaths? And we laughed?

Today, I invite you to consider that you decide when 'the end' has come for anything in your life that no longer aligns. That your beginnings and endings don't rely on a calendar.

Ask your heart: what needs to end today? What needs to begin?

DECEMBER 12, 2020

12/12

Do you follow numerology, or have you heard of Angel numbers?

Have you experienced seeing repeated number sequences say, on the clock, a sign or license plate?

This experience is commonly known as the Angels trying to get your attention, and the numbers themselves have various significance. Similarly, there is a meaning for each number in numerology. In this piece I have focused on the Angel number teaching.

When I noticed that today was 12/12 (December 12th), I knew I had to look up the meaning.

The message is that we are to focus on creating our realities with faith and trust in serving ourselves and our soul mission.

We are encouraged to release fears and apprehensions and to get on with our true path.

We are the creators of our reality.

We attract our experiences. Yes. All of them.

When you take time to focus on the positives, gratitude, the silver linings, the moments in time that light your way, you establish a different type of bond between you and the Universe. You are showing the Universe that you are operating at a certain frequency and therefore, you create the energy that will manifest more wonder, beauty and divine support in your life.

If you feel that you haven't been 'getting what you want,' you might want to consider what you've been focusing on lately. The Universe is very literal.

Pro tip: what you focus on, expands. If you're giving any attention to what you *don't want* or *what you don't have*, you'll create more lack.

Don't be too surprised if you happen to see 12/12 in your travels today. It might be confirmation to explore this teaching a little further.

DECEMBER 13, 2020

PEACE

Peace comes when we remember [at the soul level] that only Love is real.

When we get caught up in judgments and seeing things at the surface level, we create agitation in our lives. The more we look at the world through the lens of love, the more peace we create.

I wonder what would happen if we tried 'letting people off the hook' instead of carrying them around in our mind and letting them poison our peace?

Yes, even that person who cut you off in traffic.

DECEMBER 14, 2020

STANDARDS

I used to hold myself to high standards. Everything had to be perfect. Zero glitches.

Time and maturity would show me that I was not only exhausting myself, but everyone else as well because I held others to a certain standard of expectations too.

I realized I was emulating people in my past, thereby alienating myself from wonderful people and alienating 'perfectly imperfect me' from myself.

When I see people struggling with unrealistic expectations and holding others to an impossible set of standards, I know two things:

1) This person is very unhappy, and

2) Nothing and no one else will ever be enough for them.

Who are you trying to please? No one matters. I know that might be tough to digest, so I'll say it again: no one matters. Whoever you think you're trying to 'please,' you will never please them simply because you are sitting in a lack mentality, thinking that you aren't pleasing them.

Today, I want you to know that you are loved by, approved by, and supported by The Great Mystery/God/Source/Universe/Creator (whichever title you prefer).

There is no competition.

There is no list of standards.

You are good enough and that is plenty.

DECEMBER 15, 2020

MIND GREMLINS

Oh, how the Mind Gremlins take over. We prepare ourselves to learn how to do something or try to remember something we used to do from long ago. But we just can't get it. Or in my case as a writer, I doubt what I am creating.

I experience this daily. Yes. Daily.

The days when I think 'wow, this particular piece is absolute trash' is the one that resonates the most with people and I receive beautiful feedback on.

Every single time.

Mind Gremlins. They take over. They tell us all kinds of silly things, leading to self-doubt, not-good-enough-ness and an orchestra of other lies.

One thing I know with certainty, is that no matter how hard my Mind Gremlins try to state their case, there is always someone who shows up in my life to share the impact of an experience they had with me. Or a moment in time when someone smiles and I realize that just sharing space with them, is what we both needed.

Notice your Mind Gremlins today, but don't let them play. Let them know you see them and hear them, but that you're not available for their games. Then keep reminding them whenever they show up that you're not available to play.

Eventually, over time, you'll feel better about noticing them and become more amused by them than anything else.

Your Mind Gremlins will become Miracle Moments.

DECEMBER 16, 2020

GIVE YOURSELF THE GIFT OF GRACE

We have such little patience for ourselves.

Such a lack of compassion.

We pile on the demands and requirements.

To-do lists and chores.

Then if we are unwell, feeling slightly off or perhaps running on too little sleep because for some reason we couldn't settle ourselves the night before, we get bent out of shape.

We might start name-calling ourselves, saying that we are stupid for not having something go a certain way or how dumb we are for forgetting an ingredient in a meal. Ask me how I know.

When we are pushing too hard, expecting too much, or piling a load on ourselves that we would never expect anyone else to carry, we set ourselves up for disappointment. Rather than the gift of grace, we curate self-resentment which, in turn, leads to less getting done because we aren't in the mindset to do it.

Give yourself the gift of grace. You've been too hard on yourself for far too long about something or another, I'm sure of it.

It's okay to be gentler, softer and kinder to yourself. It's okay to pause and only get to one thing on your task list, just as it is okay to move through a day with simplicity and ease and wrap up ten things on your list.

If you were to allow the gift of grace to guide you today, how differently would your day look? How would you feel?

DECEMBER 17, 2020

DIVINELY DETOURED

When you *think* things have gone awry...

What if instead you considered that you are being divinely detoured?

Away from a situation that would have been harmful, unhelpful, or unnecessary had you continued going in the direction you were headed based on your original plan.

A while ago, a Shaman and one of my very dear friends said to me 'Heather, Spirit will never set you up to fail.'

I have probably repeated that phrase thousands of times to people when they are struggling with something.

Yes, even the things we question and wonder 'why.'

Even the painful stuff.

The hard stuff.

The unsettling stuff.

All of it, part of a greater plan.

This used to anger me.

Frustrate me.

Make me rebel against the falsehood of control.

Now, I see it as an opportunity to deepen my ability to surrender into trusting that I don't need to worry about the dreaded hows or the cursed whys anymore.

I have far too much living to do, don't you?

DECEMBER 18, 2020

WHAT WOULD LOVE DO?

Whatever it is you're struggling with, questioning or unsure of right now, try asking yourself: what would Love do?

What is the path, the direction, the guidance that Love would give you?

Unconditional.

Judgment-free.

Kind.

Gracious.

Forgiving.

Now, ask yourself a second question: are you doing these Loving things for you?

DECEMBER 19, 2020

UNDERREACT

I know it may be hard to imagine the impossible dream of underreacting, but what if I promised it would make you feel better if you tried?

Just sit back, let whatever is unfolding unfold and not react.

I don't mean to say that you should become a doormat or not speak up when needed.

This is about examining if you need to react to things. The phrase 'pick your battles' may help contextualize this.

So, try it today, how would you feel if you underreacted to anything that would have normally caused you to get all fired up?

DECEMBER 20, 2020

BE THE REASON PEOPLE BELIEVE THERE IS GOOD IN THE WORLD

I was thinking maybe you'd try something. Perhaps send a message to a loved one or reach out to someone you know could use a friendly hello. Maybe pay for the coffee of the person in the line behind you and start a pay-it-forward chain.

I know the world is a heavy, intense place from time to time.

I know things can be uncomfortable, disappointing and loaded with chaos.

I also believe that we are surrounded by good people more often than not.

That people care.

That hearts are big, beautiful and giving.

That there is more good in the world, than there is 'not so good.'

What small act of kindness will you choose today without expectation, other than to know you're leading with a good heart?

DECEMBER 21, 2020

WINTER SOLSTICE

Today, in the northern hemisphere, we welcome the light back into our world.

Although it may not seem to be so, it is the start of the days becoming longer and the nights becoming shorter.

It is a time to shine a light on our inner world, reflect and unearth anything that may need some attention.

It is also a time to release all that which is no longer needed or helpful in our lives.

It is time to go quiet and seek respite in the silence.

Take some time to slow down today, ease your mind, body and soul. Let yourself receive the nourishing comfort that the quiet offers and maybe do it again tomorrow (or maybe for the next three months if you can swing it).

You've done so much, dear one; you have permission to rest.

DECEMBER 22, 2020

THE FUTURE IS ALWAYS FULL OF POSSIBILITY

Each moment is the future.

Each second is a chance to explore another possibility.

I know this can be hard to trust, but it's true.

The future is now…and now…and now.

Let the experience of yesterday be released so that you can open your hands to the miracle and magic of today.

DECEMBER 23, 2020

QUIET

If your brain was a computer connected to the internet, how many tabs would it have open?

Would you know which one is nattering away with all that noise?

Would you be able to hear the silent whispers of the soul?

Would you know which direction to go when you feel as if you're being pulled in all of them?

Do you remember what quiet sounds like?

Or perhaps, feels like?

Take a moment to invite silence into your heart space and slow everything to a crawl.

As the thoughts race through your mind, witness them like train cars, one by one.

Ker-klunk. Ker-klunk. Ker-klunk. Along the track they go.

Knowing that you don't have to hitch a ride if you don't want to.

Knowing that you can observe them as they go by.

Then, as the final train car thought slips out of view, it gets quieter and quieter.

Sit in this silence for as long as you can.

You've listened to plenty, you've heard so much, you've been inundated with noise.

Allow the silence to gift you the peace that your soul silently calls for.

DECEMBER 24, 2020

COURAGE

Once upon a time, someone responded to something I'd written saying "because you are you."

It makes me think of the courage it takes to be ourselves; to see our magic when it goes against what others might expect of us or what we expect of ourselves, due to our conditioning.

I acknowledge that there are 'tried-and-true' methods for everything, but what if you're someone who doesn't fit into that category and it just doesn't work for you?

We must remember that when we try to do things the only way we've been shown, we shove ourselves into boxes and usually stunt our potential to expand, heal and learn.

Will you be courageous today?

Will you peek at what may be beyond the way you've always done something?

What's the worst that can happen? It'll either work amazingly in a way you never expected, or your 'tried-and-true' method will be re-affirmed.

Either way, you win because you are leading with the courage to be you.

DECEMBER 25, 2020

ERRORS

The other day as I was reading a newsletter from someone who has a large following, within it I noticed several errors. I thought 'Wow! You're a highly respected person in the eyes of many… my goodness, how could you make these errors?'

A few moments later, I realized that I had made an error in my latest publicly posted message, as well as in my first published book and quite possibly in this book too, which I will no doubt find after I've approved the final proof.

Well, hello, life lesson on judging others.

It reminded me that we all make errors. That we can be quick to judge and it's unnecessary, and unkind. I also realized that this was due to how I was treated around the topic of errors.

I still shudder when I think of these moments that I experienced as a child and as an adult.

Errors and the fear of errors kept me hiding for a long time. Whenever I made a mistake, I was corrected and told that mistakes were not permitted. That errors would not be accepted!

It was perfect or it was nothing!

As I reflected on this memory, I came to a couple of conclusions:

1) I need to work on how often I judge situations unfairly, and

2) I need to lead with compassion for myself and others.

I realized that when I wrote my particular 'errored' message, I was exhausted that day. I was trying to get quite a bit of work done and I wasn't as relaxed as I normally would be when I am composing work for others to receive.

I thought about the person who sent their newsletter. I wondered how they would handle it on their side. Would they be judged? Would they laugh about it? Would they worry? Would they have self-compassion?

Errors are signposts for us to pause, center ourselves and take things one step at a time.

They are a reminder to slow down and breathe.

So let's breathe.

DECEMBER 26, 2020

YOU WIN

Just remember: no matter what is going on, the Universe wants to see you win. What would someone who wins do differently today? Then maybe again tomorrow and the day after that?

Winning doesn't necessarily mean big prizes.

Winning means feeling good, maybe even proud of yourself for something.

Winning can mean something small, like not getting a coffee drip on your white shirt.

Winning could even be something a little bigger, like not reacting when someone is having a little hissy fit over something and trying to bring you into it.

Winning is whatever you choose.

Let yourself embody winning and see what that energy creates for you.

DECEMBER 27, 2020

PUSH! HARDERRRRRRR! FINISH STRONG! HOW ABOUT NO.

Last I checked we weren't giving birth or in the middle of a curling match.

Are you tired of all the ads, marketing, and sales too?

I am not 'finishing' 2020 strong.

I am not starting 2021 fiercely and 'on the right foot' to make sure I 'get it right!' and make the 'most of my year.' My goodness - there are 365 days (just like every year and a bonus day every 4th year) and we can begin in a way that feels most true to us.

I've learned I'm no longer the 'hustle' person. I used to be, and I did a fine job of it, but not anymore.

Wisdom and years of experience have taught me a few things about pushing, finishing strong and perfecting the start.

I'm allowing myself to be in this quiet space of solitude as often as possible.

I'm drinking coffee in bed in the morning.

I'm writing.

I'm reading beautiful books.

I'm not looking at my phone and I'm refusing to check emails until much later in the day.

I am pacing myself, taking it a day at a time, a minute at a time and staying in my body and as grounded as possible.

I think I may have stared out the window for nearly an hour today, just because I could.

Are you gracefully allowing yourself to 'be'? Or are you caught up in what the world is trying to demand of you?

DECEMBER 28, 2020

ENERGETIC FOCUS

If there's one thing people would say about me, it's that gratitude is a central theme in my life and the work I do.

The way I work with gratitude is the same way I work with anything: understanding that it is part of the whole picture.

You see, some will teach that you can't hold gratitude and sadness at the same time. I say you can; it just means your energetic focus is shared.

What this means is that whatever your dominant feeling or focus is, that is where your energy will be and you will feel it the most. Guess what? That's okay. Unless you're not okay with how you're feeling.

You're allowed to have sadness and you're allowed to have gratitude at the same time.

You're allowed to laugh one moment and be a sniffling-nose-hot-mess the next.

I recently received news that a very important friend, teacher, and soul-sister of mine had transitioned and is now Spirit-side. My human self is mourning this loss as she was the first person who showed me acceptance and allowed me to fully be me and helped me on my path to being public about being an Intuitive Healer.

My Spirit, my knowing-Soul, is at absolute peace and the depth of my gratitude for her and our experience cannot be put into words (said the writer).

Some teach that gratitude means you're denying the truth of a situation. A 'fake it til ya make it' kind of thing which makes me cringe.

Some teach that if you only had more gratitude, you'd be happier. Easy to say when everything feels like it's going sideways, right?

My Feather message for today is that there is no right or wrong; that various teachers connect with various students and different models and beliefs exist for a reason.

What this means is that we have permission to decide how much energetic focus we'd like to give to any emotion or experience.

No one else decides for us. We get to choose.

May your energetic focus be one way you listen to what your heart needs today.

DECEMBER 29, 2020

JUST BEGIN.

"The best time to plant a tree was 20 years ago. The second best time is now." - Chinese Proverb.

People sometimes say things like 'there isn't enough time left' or 'it's too late to begin' or they comment that they wished they had done something sooner. The truth is we need to just get to it. Whatever 'it' is that we want different.

There's nothing wrong with comfort zones and familiarity, unless you're not getting the desired results for something you're trying to achieve, do or improve upon.

I wish I had started many things decades ago too, or even last month, but I didn't. Looking back doesn't help my future. The only thing that can help my future, and my today, is if I just begin. Allowing myself to have grace, patience and self-forgiveness for the things that I, too, have put off for far too long.

Is there anything you've been putting off that would improve some aspect of your life?

No matter how big or how small, if it's in your heart, it's there for a reason.

The best time is now, so begin. Even if that beginning is forgiveness for having not started yet.

DECEMBER 30, 2020

WHO DO YOU BELIEVE IN?

A lifetime ago when I worked at an addiction treatment centre, I met some of the most pained people I had ever set eyes on. As their days in treatment went on, you'd soon see a smile come across their face; their head would be held up a little higher, they'd be the first to volunteer to help with something and they might even share a little more in a group session.

What I came to learn was that there was a key ingredient necessary that would come out in many conversations with these folks.

They realized that we believed in them when many others didn't and especially when they didn't believe in themselves.

I think the greatest gift we can give anyone is Believing in them.

Today, I want you to know that I Believe in you.

DECEMBER 31, 2020

ENDINGS AND BEGINNINGS

I'm not sure which feather was more challenging to write. The first or now this one, the last. So it is with other beginnings and endings. Sometimes we don't know how to start, sometimes we don't know how to end.

Here we are on the final December Feather which also happens to be New Year's Eve. A time when we put so much pressure on ourselves to make sure we wrap things up and prepare ourselves to start things right once the clock strikes midnight.

I'm not a resolution making kinda gal. I believe that beginnings and endings are a circle. Endings represent beginnings and all beginnings eventually become endings of some kind.

If we let ourselves gracefully glide through these moments in time and do the best we can in any given situation, we remember that it is the journey that is most important; not how it began, how it may end and most certainly not by the date on the calendar.

Give yourself permission to choose your beginnings and endings as your heart guides you.

May your days and moments ahead be filled with feather-like signs and may you choose to believe that they are a divinely guided message for you to receive.

ACKNOWLEDGEMENTS

First and foremost, thank you to you, dear reader, for choosing this book as your next read.

To all of my supporters and clients who continue to encourage and empower me to keep sharing my work.

Danielle Clarke, for her friendship, editing skills, and cheerleading.

My husband for everything, always.

Pinto, the cat, for reminding me to take breaks as he effortlessly manages to make it inconvenient for me to work.

ABOUT THE AUTHOR

After two decades of working in a typical corporate environment, Heather decided it was time to act on her exit plan. She had lived a double life for too long and chose to take her 'secret side gig' to the next level, go public, and open her healing practice full time as an Intuitive Healer, Channeler and Spiritual Guide.

For nearly a decade, Heather has helped people navigate their way through the muddled moments of life and align with their true path ahead. She helps integrate the foggy puzzle pieces, while guiding people to cultivate feelings of balance, peace and confidence. She gets up every day looking forward to being of service, but only after coffee and her quiet time sitting in session with Spirit.

She lives with her husband and their fur-kid-cat Pinto in Ontario, Canada.

Another book by Heather is *A Tiny Book About Gratitude: A Simple Practice with Superpower Strength*. You can visit her website for purchasing options.